Blue Ribbon Anima

SHOWING HORSES AT THE FAIR

I0795301

Gareth Stevens PUBLISHING

By Jennifer Wendt

Please visit our website, www.garethstevens.com. For a free color catalog of all our high-quality books, call toll free 1-800-542-2595 or fax 1-877-542-2596.

Library of Congress Cataloging-in-Publication Data

Names: Wendt, Jennifer, author.
Title: Showing horses at the fair / Jennifer Wendt.
Description: New York : Gareth Stevens Publishing, [2019] | Series: Blue ribbon animals | Includes index.
Identifiers: LCCN 2018029557| ISBN 9781538229293 (library bound) | ISBN 9781538232880 (paperback) | ISBN 9781538232897 (6 pack)
Subjects: LCSH: Horse shows--Juvenile literature. | Livestock exhibitions--Juvenile literature.
Classification: LCC SF294.7 .W46 2019 | DDC 636.1/0811--dc23
LC record available at https://lccn.loc.gov/2018029557

First Edition

Published in 2019 by
Gareth Stevens Publishing
111 East 14th Street, Suite 349
New York, NY 10003

Copyright © 2019 Gareth Stevens Publishing

Designer: Katelyn E. Reynolds
Editor: Emily Mahoney

Photo credits: Cover, p. 1 (horse) marijonas/Shutterstock.com; cover, p. 1 (background photo) chainarong06/Shutterstock.com; cover, p. 1 (blue banner) Kmannn/Shutterstock.com; cover, pp. 1-24 (wood texture) Flas100/Shutterstock.com; pp. 2-24 (paper) Peter Kotoff/Shutterstock.com; p. 5 Vasyl Syniuk/Shutterstock.com; p. 7 (western) Ahturner/Shutterstock.com; p. 7 (English) horsemen/Shutterstock.com; p. 9 Osetrik/Shutterstock.com; p. 11 Lucian Milasan/Shutterstock.com; p. 12 Frau Cosmic/Shutterstock.com; p. 13 AnnaElizabeth photography/Shutterstock.com; p. 15 JasonDoiy/E+/Getty Images; p. 17 jesadaphorn/Shutterstock.com; p. 19 taylon/Shutterstock.com; p. 21 © iStockphoto.com/BrandyTaylor.

All rights reserved. No part of this book may be reproduced in any form without permission in writing from the publisher, except by a reviewer.

Printed in the United States of America

CPSIA compliance information: Batch #CW19GS: For further information contact Gareth Stevens, New York, New York at 1-800-542-2595.

CONTENTS

*Words in the glossary appear in **bold** type the first time they are used in the text.*

GET READY TO RIDE!

Horses are beautiful animals, and showing them at your local fair is a fun way for you to learn all about them. From different styles of riding to training your horse, there's a lot to learn about making your horse into a blue ribbon winner.

Showing any animal takes a lot of time and hard work. But in the end, you'll make new friends, have a great time, and even learn something along the way!

Get to know your horse well, and maybe you'll bring home a ribbon from the fair!

CHOICES TO MAKE

In a horse show, there are two main riding styles: English and Western. You'll need to decide what riding **competition** you want to enter in order to start training. In Western riding, the **saddle** is bigger and more comfortable. It also has a horn in front for you to hold onto. Western riders sometimes wear a cowboy hat and cowboy boots.

In English riding, the saddle is smaller and lighter. Riders wear a fitted jacket and tall boots. Some people think English riding takes more practice to learn.

WESTERN RIDING

Check out the differences between English and Western riding styles. Which one would you like to try?

ENGLISH RIDING

TAKE THE PRIZE!

ENGLISH RIDERS OFTEN WEAR A COAT, SHIRT, **JODHPURS**, BOOTS, AND A HELMET. WESTERN RIDERS OFTEN WEAR A SHIRT, TIE, BELT, JEANS, BOOTS, AND A HELMET.

START YOUR TRAINING

Once you choose your riding style, it's time to start training! It's important to work with your horse several times a week. If you're a beginner, make sure to have an adult nearby in case you need help.

Reading your fair guide will tell you what the judges will be looking for. This will help you train with your horse. If you know what to expect, you and your horse will be relaxed on the day you show at the fair.

TAKE THE PRIZE!

HORSES ARE VERY SMART ANIMALS, SO IT'S IMPORTANT TO KEEP THEM BUSY WITH TOYS SO THEY DON'T GET BORED.

Having a large ball to play with will keep your horse busy and happy.

GETTING YOUR HORSE READY

Keeping your horse healthy at home and at the fair is important. Find out what **vaccinations** your horse needs before you go. Keep any paperwork with you to show the fair officials.

Just like you, your horse will need a ride to the fair. Practice loading and unloading your horse into the trailer so he doesn't get scared when it's time to go. You may need to give your horse a treat to help him to walk into the trailer!

TAKE THE PRIZE!

HORSES CAN SLEEP LYING DOWN AND STANDING UP. YOUR HORSE MIGHT EVEN TAKE A NAP ON THE WAY TO THE FAIR!

Let your horse get used to the trailer before the ride to the fair.

GROOMING YOUR HORSE

When you **groom** your horse, you're not only making him look nice, you're also building trust. Some of the tools you'll need are brushes, a face cloth, a hoof pick, and a comb. Groom your horse before and after riding.

Right before the fair, give your horse a bath. Use whitening shampoo if your horse has any white spots. Don't forget to clean your horse's ears, eyes, nose, and hooves. You'll be judged on how your horse looks!

HOOF PICK

You want to make sure your horse looks his best for the fair!

CLEAN YOUR TACK

You should take some time before the show to clean your tack. Tack is what you use to ride your horse, such as a saddle and **bridle**. You'll want to make sure your tack is clean and in good shape before you head to the fair.

Wipe down your horse's saddle and bridle, and check for any cracks, rips, or broken **buckles**. Remember where the buckles on the bridle were set so it will still fit your horse the right way after you clean it.

TAKE THE PRIZE!

STORE YOUR TACK IN A COOL, DRY PLACE TO KEEP IT IN GREAT SHAPE.

You and your horse both need to look your best in the show-ring. The judges will score you on your tack, too!

GOING TO THE FAIR

It's time to go to the fair! Grab all your tack, grooming tools, horse food, and show clothes and load your horse into the trailer. Don't forget your vaccination records and fair **registration papers.** When you arrive at the fairgrounds, check in and find your **stall.** Give your horse clean **bedding** and fresh food and water.

If possible, bring your horse to the show-ring. Get your horse used to the space so he can do his best later on while you're being judged.

Keep your horse's stall clean. It's his home away from home!

SHOW-RING ROUNDUP

When it's time for you to show your horse, check that your clothes are clean. Always wear a helmet when you're riding. Look the judges in the eye and answer questions about your horse clearly.

Stay calm and don't worry if something goes wrong. If you stay calm, your horse will too. Showing your horse is about control, so show the judges how well you and your horse work together. Remember, you've practiced for this!

It's important to look your best in the show-ring!

UNTIL NEXT YEAR

When your time in the show-ring is over, thank the judges and return your horse to his stall. Hopefully you'll be going home with a ribbon! Not everyone wins a ribbon, but showing your horse at the fair is still lots of fun!

After the fair, clean out your stall and pack up your grooming tools and tack. Don't forget to thank everyone who helped you get ready for the fair. Finally, load your horse into the trailer for the ride home.

TAKE THE PRIZE!

IF YOU HAVE THE CHANCE TO TALK TO THE JUDGES, ASK THEM WHAT YOU DID WELL AND WHAT YOU COULD DO BETTER. YOU'LL HAVE A HEAD START FOR NEXT YEAR!

Hard work and practice could earn you and your horse a blue ribbon!

GLOSSARY

bedding: matter used for an animal's bed, such as straw, newspaper, or wood shavings

bridle: a device that fits on a horse's head and that is used for guiding and controlling the horse

buckle: a metal or plastic part that is attached to one end of a belt or strap and that is used to connect it to the other end

competition: an event in which people try to win

groom: to clean

jodhpurs: tight pants that are worn for horseback riding

registration papers: an official record of information

saddle: a leather-covered seat that is put on the back of a horse

stall: an enclosed area in a building where a farm animal, such as a horse or cow, is kept

vaccination: a shot that keeps a person or animal from getting a certain sickness

For More Information

BOOKS

Bodden, Valerie. *Showing Horses*. Mankato, MN: Creative Paperbacks, 2014.

Gibbs, Maddie. *Horses*. New York, NY: PowerKids Press, 2015.

Simon, Seymour. *Horses*. New York, NY: Harper Collins, 2017.

WEBSITES

4-H
4-h.org
4-H gives children a chance to learn new skills through hands-on projects.

Horseback Riding
www.dkfindout.com/us/sports/horseback-riding/
Visit this website for fun facts about horseback riding.

National FFA Organization
www.ffa.org
Future Farmers of America is an education-based organization for students interested in farming.

Publisher's note to educators and parents: Our editors have carefully reviewed these websites to ensure that they are suitable for students. Many websites change frequently, however, and we cannot guarantee that a site's future contents will continue to meet our high standards of quality and educational value. Be advised that students should be closely supervised whenever they access the internet.

INDEX